Adva
*Just What the Doctor Ordered*

You will enjoy this inspiring and motivating book on living your best and fullest life after discovering your soul's purpose. Dr. Kelechi urges you to step away from limitations and live the very achievable life of your dreams. And just as most prescriptions need to be taken again and again to work most effectively, this book will lead to the most transformation if you read it and internalize the message multiple times! Go ahead: read, absorb the message and apply just what the doctor ordered!

— Kemunto Mokaya, MD, FAAD (Dr. Kemmy), board-certified dermatologist, author, and speaker.

I found this book well thought through and well written. We are all athletes running toward our goals and it is a great comfort to know that one does not have to run this race alone. In this must-read book, Dr. Kelechi lays out a step-by-step plan to help you overcome limiting beliefs and break through to your next level. She also includes summary points at the back of each chapter for those who want a quick read. How badly do you need a breakthrough? Take the next step and get this book…your journey awaits.

— Dr. Omerine, MD, family doctor, lifestyle medicine specialist, and faith-based life transformation coach

The first line in chapter one of Dr. Kelechi Uduhiri's fabulous book *Just What the Doctor Ordered* is a quote from Helen Keller: "What I'm looking for is not out there, it is in me." What a perfect introduction to a book that provides step-by-step instructions on how to transition to a person living their life with intention. Achieving that goal is not necessarily intuitive or easy for an individual but Dr. Uduhiri's book provides the perfect roadmap with detailed commentary followed by an exercise for readers to complete and implement. This book touches on the basic principles needed to achieve purposeful living and if applied correctly will undoubtedly be an asset to the reader.

—Randi B. Nelson, MD, MBA

Dr. Kelechi Uduhiri is both my friend, confidant, and esteemed colleague. She invites us all to come on a life changing journey in her book, *Just What the Doctor Ordered*. From the beginning of this important book to its ending, infused with her compassion, insight and kindness, you will find not only Dr. Kelechi, you will also find yourself! She takes us on a journey that begins in her native land in Nigeria to Vienna, Austria, and then on to her medical education in the United States. A truly global citizen, she quite literally is good medicine for anyone, especially women who need to get out of their own way and truly lead a fulfilling life. Yes, I couldn't agree more when Dr. Kelechi urges us to live our best life now.

Each chapter ends with a life enhancing, life affirming summary with actionable steps to begin using immediately to live your best life now. Dr. Kelechi repeats a very powerful question in her book: "What is your next best step for making the transition into your new self? I can't begin to tell you which idea or which step I enjoyed the most, you will just have to get the book and take the journey for yourself!

— Carol A. Penn, DO, MA, ABOM, FACOFP, author of the
bestselling book *Meditation in a Time of Madness*


Dr. Kelechi is the epitome of successful transformation. She is a true leader who has successfully integrated being a practicing physician and serial entrepreneur while coaching others to greatness. I am so grateful she has consolidated just a portion of her wealth of experience and knowledge in this engaging and insightful book. It is a must-read for anyone making any type of life transition.

— Sylvia Gonsahn-Bollie, MD, obesity medicine specialist,
ABOM, internal medicine/ primary care, ABIM


Dr. Kelechi challenges the notions of what we think we are "supposed to have," how we're "supposed to" feel about what we have, and gives us permission to redefine our success in a way that serves our spirit. Her approach is one of sincerity and optimism. She understands the power that comes from the vulnerability in letting your trials shape you, and is a testament to the reward that lies on the other side.

—Dr. Stacy Cary-Thompson, MD, FAAP, pediatrics

Dr. Kelechi knows who she is. In *Just What the Doctor Ordered*, she describes her lifelong journey to her own personal understanding. Now she is sharing her gifts with the world. Her inspiring story takes the reader through her childhood in Nigeria with parents who nurtured her passion for service and excellence and ultimately made the choice to send her to the United States. She is unapologetic about her values and positions that are founded in faith. Her personal journey continues now with another calling to spread her truth to help others. You will be moved by her story, inspired by her faith, and amazed at what she has accomplished on her most recent journey. Spread throughout the book are useful tips for anyone on their own journey. She is generous with her teaching. Don't make the mistake of underestimating Dr. Kelechi. I can't wait to see what she does next!

— Susan Douglas, MD, JD, author, policymaker, healthcare and disability advocate, assistant adjunct professor at UCLA School of Medicine, CEO of Douglas Consulting, LLC

In summary, this book is a total reflection of the person we all know as Dr. Kelechi. She found out very early on the purpose of living—to make this world a better place while you are here and upon leaving, not for yourself, but for humanity. *Just What the Doctor Ordered* is a playbook on how to accomplish this onerous task. First and foremost, Dr. Kelechi makes us all realize that each of us is born with certain talents, but what lacks for most of us is how to extract it from our inner self and make it useful. Once you have discovered it, then there is no limit to what you can accomplish in life. Some big lessons, or as she calls them, mantras, are being flexible in your learning, listening to your inner self, and never settling for what you already know, but keep reaching out for the unknowns. She teaches us to not be fearful of failure that will make us not try. It is indeed the risk takers and folks thinking outside the box who are called pioneers who make this world a whole lot better for all of us like Dr. Kelechi.

— Sohail Qarni, MD, MPH, FAAFP, State of Maryland, medical director of the Prevention and Health Promotion Administration

This is hands down one of the most inspiring books I have ever read, and I highly recommend it to anyone looking for inspiration to transform their lives successfully. Hooray and congratulations to my friend Dr. Kelechi Uduhiri for writing such an amazing book!

—Zena Jalloh, MD, emergency medicine

It is my greatest pleasure to provide commentary for this truly fabulous book by my dear friend Dr. Kelechi Uduhiri. In weaving through the ten reasons for making the transition into your new self, Dr. Uduhiri's *Just What the Doctor Ordered* not only takes the reader through her personal journey, but will inspire the reader to reflect on his/her own. This book challenges you to make your own changes by giving step-by-step guidance on how to achieve your goals, beginning with formulating a vision through self-reflection and defining core values through letting go of preconceived and limiting notions. Dr. Uduhiri pushes the reader to seek the freedom to meet one's goals and finally reach the point to where one's decisions and actions serve to nourish the soul. The selected quotes and motivational exercises also help the reader put a plan into action and then start their own journey.

—Dr. Nana Atta-Asamoah, MD,
family medicine, geriatrician

# Just What the Doctor Ordered

# Just What the Doctor Ordered

**Ten Reasons to Live Your Truth**

KELECHI A. UDUHIRI,
MD, MPH, MS

publish
your gift

# JUST WHAT THE DOCTOR ORDERED

Special discounts are available on bulk quantity purchases by book clubs, associations and special interest groups. For details email: sales@publishyourgift.com or call (888) 949-6228. *For information logon to:* www.PublishYourGift.com

*As long as I am in the world,*
*I am the light of the world.*

John 9:5

*To my five siblings, Ebere, Oluchi, Chinyere, Uchechi, and Udochukwu; and my parents, my late father Isaiah Chidi Nnaji and loving mother Juliana Nwakaego Nnaji. Thank you for being my Why and my inspiration. Thank you for teaching me excellence, expecting excellence, and demonstrating excellence. I am because you believe in me. I hope this book inspires you as you have inspired me.*

# TABLE OF CONTENTS

# ACKNOWLEDGMENTS

I always find it challenging to write an acknowledgment page because there are countless individuals to thank. My family and friends, both locally and globally, who faithfully walked with me on this journey of life and believed in me when I did not believe in myself. The countless students, mentors, teachers, and colleagues that have certainly shaped my worldview and allowed me to grow into the person that I am today. The thousands of patients I have had the privilege to serve over nearly two decades of practicing medicine have undoubtedly left an indelible impression on me and taught me countless times the importance of humility as well as lessons in servant leadership.

I acknowledge my God, my ancestors on whose shoulders I rise, my parents and five siblings whose love, support, and encouragement allowed me to flourish. The list cannot be contained on this page, and I acknowledge you all. I must also thank Hannah Gordon and Susan Morrison for their editing. Editors play a pivotal part in bringing the best of writers forth, and this book reflects their altruistic efforts and talents. I would also like to thank Publish Your Gift for the cover design and for the layout.

I would like to gratefully acknowledge the contribution of four unique and special individuals who provided invaluable assistance in making this manuscript a reality. First, thanks to my husband, Loveday Uduhiri, for his sincere words of encouragement, giving up countless hours to brainstorm with me and helping me to organize my thoughts. And to Elizabeth Muna, the senior national sales director with Mary Kay Cosmetics for her belief, inspiration, and always encouraging me to dream big. To Dr. Carol Penn, my soul sister, and a successful author in her own right, who allowed her light to shine and paved the way for me to discover the author in me. Last but certainly not least, my business coach, Dr. Draion Burch, for your commitment to excellence and giving me all the tools and structure I needed to thrive beyond my own belief and publish this book!

# INTRODUCTION

*I was once afraid of people saying,*
*"Who does she think she is?" Now I have the courage*
*to stand and say, "This is who I am."*

—Oprah Winfrey

My story begins in the small but mighty West African country of Nigeria where I was born. I witnessed dilapidated rural clinics and ill-equipped city hospitals. I was forever changed by seeing the impacts of poverty and the lack of a public healthcare system on the overall well-being of individuals and communities. Fortunately, my parents were hardworking and well educated. My father was a teacher, a mathematician, and a philanthropist. My mother was an elementary school teacher and a businesswoman.

A promotion for my father into the diplomatic service meant that my family would relocate to Europe. For the next nine years, I grew up in Vienna, Austria, learned to speak German and French, and traveled with my parents and four sisters. I attended the best private school with my siblings. My father worked as a statistician with OPEC (Organization of Petroleum Exporting Countries) and my mother was a stay-at-home mom. While raising five daughters, she went to school at night to earn her business degree. In Vienna, we had the privilege of a family physician who made house calls and took care of our entire family. I experienced the best health-care. Our family physician diagnosed my nearly ruptured appendix in his office; he visited me in the hospital, and he made post-operative visits to our home. I wanted to be that kind of doctor—the kind that took care of the family and followed the patient from illness to wellness! I eventually immigrated to the United States to further my education and pursue my dream of becoming a doctor.

Prior to becoming a physician, I studied biology and earned my bachelor of science degree from the University of Maryland. My interest in public health led to earning my master of public health (MPH) from The George Washington University. While at GWU, I worked for three years as a research associate in the epidemiology field with a consulting firm in Washington, DC. What a great start to my primary and public health career! From there, I finally went on to medical school and graduated from Rutgers-Robert Wood Johnson Medical School. I became the first in my family to earn a doctoral degree and to become a physician. I was the immigrant who came to America and achieved her American dream!

Post-graduation from medical school, I completed preventive medicine residency training at the University of

Maryland in Baltimore, where I simultaneously earned my master's degree in epidemiology. From there, I moved back to Washington, DC, and successfully completed a second specialty in family medicine at the Georgetown/Family Medicine residency program. I landed my first job straight out of residency as the medical director of a federally-qualified health center (FQHC) and on the teaching faculty in the department of Family Medicine at MedStar Franklin Square Hospital Center in Baltimore, Maryland. Over the next decade, I pursued full-spectrum family medicine-obstetrics including delivering more than 200 babies. During this time, I also had the opportunity to pursue a passion of mine: medical mission trips, which took me to Jamaica, Haiti, and back to my country of origin, Nigeria.

However, As I continued to practice both in academic and outpatient clinical settings, I began to feel that I was spending more time with paperwork, third party payers, and hospital administrators and less time with my patients and my community. Time with patients dropped to an average of seven minutes per patient, while staying up late into the night documenting electronic medical records became the norm. The hours in the clinic and hospital seemed to get longer, time with family seemed rare, the joy of being a doctor, along with my empathy, started to decline. I could not recognize the doctor I had become; I felt I had strayed away from my soul's purpose, from the family doctor I wanted to become growing up in Europe. I finally had to admit that although I loved my profession, I was not sure it loved me. Getting up in the morning to go to work became a lackluster experience and I knew this was not how I was supposed to feel. I had to admit that I was burning out!

I have always felt that I was called to greatness. I started to feel there was more to me than the four walls of medicine. In search of my soul's purpose, I discovered that aside from healing I was called to liberate others. I realized that I could accomplish that via entrepreneurship. I decided that I was going to become a mindset coach and motivational speaker to help individuals create successful home-based businesses. Why? To be home with their families, making an executive income and not sacrificing self. Which business? Business coaching for women with a focus on the self-care and skin care industry.

I wanted to empower women, and to teach them and show them how to take care of themselves. The skin care and color cosmetics industry seemed recession-proof, and I was already using a brand I loved. I had been successful in marketing the brand and built a customer base of more than 200 individuals and a team of more than 100 women. I combined this passion for entrepreneurship with my love for teaching and created Business Leaders Success Coaching Academy. My first dream was to become a physician. I found my next dream was to develop successful women business leaders globally in the skin care sector and use my financial success to become a philanthropist, building schools for girls and state-of-the art hospitals for women in West Africa.

Because of this vision, I wrote this book, and I am planning the launch of a concierge practice to include coaching individuals to wellness while empowering women to build successful home-based businesses. Living in my purpose has allowed me to coach women like me on how to use their expertise to earn an income from wherever they live, work, and play. Women deserve a lifestyle of time freedom. So my purpose in writing this book is just that, as a testimony to others, that if they can believe in themselves, they can achieve anything their heart desires. Sharing my passion for entrepreneurship means sharing what I have learned in the process with the world. What I have come to appreciate the most is the notion to live in the now; to accept the journey and the destination as one with immense gratitude manifesting countless miracles. Our gifts are not meant for us but are meant to be given away to empower others. My hope is that this book will serve as a source of inspiration to live your best life now.

# FOREWORD

As a friend and business partner, I have had the privilege to share professional and personal space with Dr. Kelechi. Readers might find satisfaction in knowing that this book is entirely written from Dr. Kelechi's real experiences. We live in a world today that makes it simple to settle in our comfort zone, especially when perceiving that one has reached an agreeable level of success ascribed by society. However, I believe that true success continues as self-discovery on the path of your soul's purpose. As we stand in our truth, owning and living in our light admits all the imperfection. We then can authentically serve others and equally give them the freedom to embrace their Light, their Soul's Purpose, if you will.

While this journey may seem like a natural progression in life, I find that it is a path that many "successful professionals" find difficult to take or stay on. It is easy to fall in the trappings of what financial security brings when one has attained a title or professional status, along with the notoriety. This state of being may sometimes stifle authenticity and organic ideas that require free thinking and creativity. This is because at this stage of success we are prone to play in the restricted confines of the norms of the corporations we work for in order to secure the job that maintains the lifestyle and social status that we enjoy. Taking this path does not necessarily mean that we lose all that we are or have. However, it requires that you think differently, with the understanding that what you define as success is a gateway to access your greater self that is limitless; hence refusing to define yourself by the norms of popularist success.

Applying the ten reasons in this book forces one to think outside limited confines and to begin to define their own understanding of success. They push us to be authentic, beyond our survival mentality and charter unchanneled waters that will guarantee self-satisfaction and fulfillment in one's life beyond physical or materialistic things. What I know is that this book sets the pathway for anyone who believes that there is more than what meets the eye in their lives but does not quite know how to get started in aligning their life work with their soul's purpose (for the real job is one's personal work). If this is you, you must read *Just What the Doctor Ordered* several times. In this book, my friend uses authentic and transparent examples, including herself. After each chapter, she includes mantras that expand the reader's mind to what is possible for a person who is ready to "transition."

There isn't a better time to read this book. For we are living in a time of change that asks us to be, to do, and to think differently as the universe realigns and organizes itself. You can be a miracle worker in this transition! Use *Just What the Doctor Ordered* as your powerful tool for your empowerment!

**Elizabeth Muna**
Senior National Sales Director, Mary Kay Inc.

# CHAPTER 1

# Vision: Creating a Life of Your Dreams. If not now, then when?

*What I'm looking for is not out there, it is in me.*

—Helen Keller

This is the moment you have been waiting for your entire life. This is the moment to cast your vision and to become the creator of your own destiny. For the only way to predict the future is to create it. Embrace it. Believe in yourself and know that that which you desire, also desires you. You are perfect in your imperfection. You are here on the Earth School to manifest your unique gifts. Take action now.

Know thyself: It is important to know that you are uniquely and wonderfully made. You were created in His image and as such no mistake was made in the process. How could your Creator make a mistake? It is impossible. Knowing whose you are is knowing that you have the blood of royalty already flowing through you. Knowing whose you are will allow you freedom to begin to accept the greatness that lies within you. You cannot fail unless you do not believe that greatness lies within you. If you accept this as fact then anything that you desire can be yours. There is no limit to what you can accomplish in life if you believe in yourself. All that is missing in your current reality is the belief that you already have that which you desire.

Ask: With the knowing that your vision was given to you for one reason only and that reason is to manifest your gifts and to share it with the world. You don't really need to ask for the sake of asking. I say this because your Creator has nothing else to give you. He created you in His image, so His creation is complete and the work is done. You simply need to say thank you God for the vision and begin one step at time, day by day with inspired action. Feel your wish fulfilled every single day and you will surely see it manifest. Know that the vision is waiting for you to show up and walk in it.

Believe: Believing in yourself is the bridge you must cross to self-actualization. Believing in yourself means that you now recognize and accept that there is greatness within you. Believing in yourself means that you are ready to bring it forth. We have been programmed through people and events in our lives that the process of manifesting our desires is enthralled in physical strength, in competition or through external forces. Nothing could be further from the truth. It starts with believing in yourself. But how? First, let go of all the negative and disempowering beliefs that you have been told about who you are. If it does not empower you and allow you to feel good about yourself, then it is not of God. You begin to believe in yourself by accepting all that your Creator says about you.

Receive: Your vision is your gift and it is up to you to receive it. You must first be willing to receive it, meaning you must see it as already yours. Do you know that your vision is who you really are and who you were meant to be all along? Do you see your vision as already yours? Everything that is seen is created twice, first in the mind and then in reality. When was the last time you stood still to imagine and see your vision, your dream in your mind's eye? Receiving is so important because it says you no longer have any fears or doubts that what is meant for you is coming to you. Can you feel just how powerful this step in seeing your dreams manifest? There was nothing wrong with dreaming as a child and there is nothing wrong with dreaming as an adult. We must never give up on our dreams because it is our Creator's desire for us to contribute that unique gift to the world and make it a better place. The dream is the Creator manifesting through you. The dream was given to you for a reason; and the reason is that you were the only one designed to deliver it to humanity. So don't give up on it. Feel it, receive it and be it.

Use your imagination: Seeing it in your mind requires using your imagination. Your imagination is where the greatness within you resides. Tap into your imagination by taking time out daily for yourself to be still. When you meditate, feel the feeling of what it would be like when your desires become your reality. This process of connecting with your desires and your dreams is needed to connect with your subconscious mind. It is needed to collapse the bridge between your vision and your reality. Remember that your vision is who you were always meant to become. That is why it is called vision. For what you see within you is what you are meant to be.

## Living My Truth by Living My Vision

I can certainly say that my personal journey of becoming a physician represents the story of the vision that I held for myself since childhood. From the early age of eight, I knew with every fiber of my being that I wanted to become a physician. I did not know then how this would come to pass. There were no physicians in my family, and I was growing up in Vienna, Austria, but attending an English school and thus, was not confident that I would gain sufficient proficiency in German to attend university and medical school there.

My passion for becoming a doctor was certainly fueled by our family physician who would make house calls to check on my family. I revered him greatly for the vast knowledge he must have had to master all our ailments. His compassion, attentiveness and genuine interest in the overall well-being of my family inspired me to become that kind of doctor. At the end of my parents' service in Vienna, Austria, I was in my mid-teens, and my parents decided to return to our home country of Nigeria. They also decided that I would not return with them.

Instead, I would immigrate to the United States to continue my education. At that time, I felt that nothing could stop me from achieving my dream. I did not experience any anxiety about the separation from my family at the time. It felt like an adventure, like the next evolution in my personal growth, like my dream was coming to pass. In retrospect, I had held and felt this vision so strongly, that out of the five children in my family, I was the one chosen to remain overseas. After fourteen years of higher education, including extensive postgraduate training, I walked into the vision that I had seen, the dream that I had dreamt, and the calling that I knew was mine, and became the first female to become a medical doctor in my family.

# Five Mantras

1. You are perfect in your imperfection.

2. There is no limit to what you can accomplish in life if you believe in yourself.

3.  Feel your wish fulfilled every single day and you will surely see it manifest.

4.  Believing in yourself means that you now recognize and accept that there is greatness within you.

5.  Your vision is who you really are and who you were meant to be all along.

# What is the next best step for making the transition into living your truth?

Use your imagination and write down all that you envision for yourself.

# CHAPTER 2

# Core Values: What are your core values, and do you live by them?

*One of the truest tests of integrity is its blunt
refusal to be compromised.*

—**Chinua Achebe**

Living your truth allows you to follow principles and ethics that are important and meaningful to you. You are now
making decisions based on your own values and not on the
values of others. Seize this opportunity to become the truest
representation of yourself. Your soul yearns for this level of
authenticity.

What are core values? Core values are tenets by which you
strive to live your life. If you were living the best version of
yourself, your core values will be reflected in all that you do.
You and your core values would be one and the same in tone,

attitude, and expression. When others describe you, they will accurately be describing your core values. Some of my core values include the words: abundant, authentic, compassion, contribution, empowerment, excellence, freedom, joy, inspiration, and leadership. Core values reflect what you stand for, how you try to live your life every day, how you make your decisions, your truest intentions, and how you define your *raison d'être*—your reason for existence. These are essential as they define how you live your daily life and create your future legacy. It is vital to think deeply about your core values and write down your own core values statement, which we'll discuss later in this chapter.

Where do core values come from? Core values come from your sense of pride in who you are and who you aspire to become. They may arise from the context of familial upbringing, cultural community and/or society, but inherently they reflect your foundational truths. These truths can also be viewed as your priorities and so it is important to reflect on what those may be and what they mean to you. Often, core values will arise from the vision that you have for yourself or your brand. How you want to be imagined or perceived in the world or marketplace should be reflected in your core values.

How do you identify your core values? Start with what you currently admire about yourself or your brand company. Decide what makes you unique or helps you to stand out in your community or marketplace. What is important to you that you are most proud of and could that be nourished and embraced? This is a good place to start with identifying your core values. Remember that your core values are your foundational truths that lie deep within you and you need not go anywhere to acquire them. List all the adjectives that those who know you would use to describe your character. What is the most frequent adjective used to describe you? This would be another approach to identifying your core values.

Do you live by your core values? You want to strive on a daily basis to live by your core values because they mirror the principles and ethics that you believe in. Your core values should reflect the spirit or ethos of who you are. People don't care as much about how much you know until they know how much you care; and thus, they will experience your essence through the way you express your core values. When you broadcast your core values, who do you attract? And do they reflect how you truly want to be known? When you do not live by your core values you will instinctively experience discomfort or dissatisfaction in decisions that you make that do not reflect your truest intention. You may need to reevaluate your core values as you grow and change. If you define your intentions with all you do, and you evaluate your intentions vis-a-vis your core values, you should feel a sense of pride and satisfaction about your decision-making process. This is how you will know that you are living by your core values.

How do you stay consistent with your core values? Being consistent with your core values will reflect what you believe in and what you stand for. Your core values should be visible at all times and will become part of your mantra—like a brand for a business. Consistency comes from daily embedding and evaluating all your decision-making through the lens of your core values. It takes effort and daily accountability to arrive at consistency but it will be worth it as you begin to set yourself apart from the masses. To whom do you hold yourself accountable? Are your habits and decisions transparent and do they reflect the image or identity which you desire to portray? If so, you are in alignment with your core values.

## Living My Core Values

As a physician, I appreciate the power of core values to keep me living in my truth. By course correcting when I've started down a path that was inconsistent with my values, I've experienced greater fulfillment in my life. For about a decade in my career as a primary care physician I held several positions. I felt that so much of what I was engaged in had little to do with care of my patients. As the documentation requirements in modern electronic health record systems grew, the time I spent in patient care began to dwindle. Quite frequently I questioned whether I was doing data care or patient care.

I truly enjoyed the time I spent with my patients, hearing about their families, and getting to understand their life stories. It not only helped my patients trust me more, but it was a great way to get good patient health history, which rendered my clinical decision-making that much easier. When I spent more time on paperwork and less time with patients, I felt entirely disconnected to why I believed I was called to serve. What are the main core values of being a family physician? For me, being a real family physician meant—and still means—being passionate about taking care of families—the way that my family doctor was when I was a child. That was the practice that I fell in love with and wanted to become a part of. How was it that after fourteen years of higher education, I could no longer recognize it in its current form in our healthcare system? In my naïveté, I felt the healthcare system owed it to me to allow me to live out these values. But I discovered and had to finally accept ten years into practice, that our broken healthcare system simply would not allow me to deliver on my core values. My idealism was tested, my spirit conflicted. The system was the system; and I had to either comply or exit.

I was extremely challenged with honoring my core values as a family physician and thus I began to feel my emotional and physical health suffer. At various times, I felt a significant amount of burnout. Feelings included fatigue, mood swings, and loss of interest in my activities. It was exercise and running that saved me. Simply staying physically active gave me the resilience I needed to bounce back and ploughed through. I turned into a half-marathon enthusiast to survive my medical career. I enjoyed running, and I needed the constant high of my endorphins to survive the deep lows of despair and un-fulfillment I would frequently go through. My patients made it worth it. Nothing like the loud shrill of a newborn's first breath to quickly reconnect me to the family medicine I knew and to remind me of why I chose to become a healer. But when the hospital where I delivered babies was forced to close its doors, traditional primary care could no longer fill the void. Understanding that it was the deviation from my core values as a family doctor and the impact of my health, that led to my dissatisfaction significantly bolstered me and gave me the courage to finally walk away from traditional medicine and to pursue medical practice in my own terms, in alignment, with my core values.

Earlier I mentioned writing your own core values state-ment. Now that you've learned what core values are, how to identify and live by them, you can write your own statement. To discover your personal core values, I highly recommend that you follow the process designed by Scott Jeffrey as a start-ing point. His seven steps provide a simple guided approach to identify your core values and to see if you live by them. By completing his exercises, you will discover that the extent to which you align to your core values will determine your qual-ity of life.

# Five Mantras

1. Core values reflect what you stand for, your truest intentions, how you live your life every day, and how you make your decisions.

2. Core values come from your sense of pride in who you are and who you aspire to become.

3. Core values are your foundational truths that lie deep within you and you need not go anywhere to acquire them.

4. You may need to reevaluate your core values as you grow and change.

5. Staying consistent with your core values will come from daily embedding and evaluating all your decision-making through the lens of your core values.

# What is the next best step for making the transition into living your truth?

Decide what makes you unique or helps you to stand out in your communities.

# CHAPTER 3

# Leading Yourself: Who said you can't have it all?

*A tiger does not shout its tigritude, it acts.*

—Wole Soyinka

You can now make decisions faster. You are in a position to empower others to lead and take control. You are creating opportunities for growth for others and inspiring them to become a better version of themselves. You will feel the satisfaction of accomplishing your goals in a record time.

Why lead yourself? Leading yourself starts with identifying your calling and finding your purpose. You will need to lead yourself when your dream or your call is so powerful that anything less than manifesting it will leave you unfulfilled. Your dream is yours and you alone are responsible for seeing it to fruition. Your dream was given to you, so therefore you are your own best resource, so learn to be self-reliant. Being self-reliant goes very well with the saying, "When the student is ready, the master will appear." Believe without questioning that all you will need to lead yourself is already within you. She or he who has the problem intrinsically has the solutions. Others may hear your call, hop on your bandwagon, take some or all of the journey with you but it is ultimately you who must lead. You will lead yourself in order to arrive at one of your many milestones of success and there will be many if you lead.

What are the characteristics of a great leader? An acronym that I created when I think of a great leader is E.P.I.C.C, which stands for Excellence, Purpose, Integrity, Courage and Compassion. A great leader strives for excellence in all that they do and is not content with the status quo. **Excellence** is simply the cornerstone and the foundation of their call to action in all that they strive to accomplish. Striving for excellence does not negate the possibility that a great leader will experience setbacks or feelings of failure. However, to be a great leader, excellence means that they are willing to grow through their so-called failures which they equate to learning. A great leader knows that there is no such thing as failure; merely challenges or stumbling blocks, if you will, which are a part of the journey of leadership. You have to grow through these challenges in order to walk others through it. A great leader appreciates that they cannot lead through what they have not gone through. Excellence means quitting is not an option and the only outcome is the goal desired.

**Purposeful** leaders have a vision that is clear and well communicated to those they lead. A leader must have vision for their people which allows those whom they lead to remain focused on the dream that is hoped for. A visionary leader sees the finish line and empowers the people to latch on to the mission and never lose sight of the goal. A visionary leader is purposeful and has mastered the art of helping others identify their purpose.

**Integrity** is another characteristic of a great leader. Their word is their bond and trust between them and those they lead must not be broken. Integrity means speaking truth to power and leaders with integrity appreciate this dialogue from those they lead. Such leaders are not afraid of criticism nor do they chastise those who challenge their authority. **Courage** is inherent in great leaders. They feel the fear of that which seems impossible or feels hopeless, yet never give up hope; never entertain the thought of defeat. Courage means having the willingness to go through trials and tribulations and allowing them to shape you into who you were meant to be. Courage is necessary to go through defeat and emerge victorious. **Compassion** for yourself on each step of the journey toward becoming a better version of you is important as it will allow you to connect spiritually with others and have compassion for them as well. The journey of leading yourself for your greater good and in turn for that of humanity begins and ends with compassion.

# How to Lead Yourself

Never lose sight of your vision, never let go of your dreams. Keep them before you and review them daily. Use positive affirmations daily to plant the seeds of belief in yourself that will continuously build you up. Your daily habits will form your work ethic which will develop your character and help you evolve into the great leader that you have aspired to become. Life circumstances including emotional, physical, environmental, or socio-economic challenges may present as a roadblock to your goals but this is when it will be most critical to lead yourself and show up anyway for your dreams. Holding yourself accountable and allowing others to hold you accountable is an effective strategy to implement whenever possible on your leadership journey. Accountability partners do not let us off the hook; they ensure that we maintain integrity with the commitments that we have made to ourselves. I use an accountability partner whenever I have a big goal, such as writing my first book! It worked.

# How to Lead Others

In 1996, *Forbes* named Mary Kay Ash as one of the greatest business stories of all time.

She once said that the best way to lead people is by example, example, example. Remember that people do not care how much you know until they know how much you care.

You want to fall in love with your people so that they will fall in love with you (Sadhguru). You are the creator of the culture of your team. How it performs is a reflection of your leadership. I truly believe that you cannot take your team to a destination where you personally have not gone or are not willing to be the first to arrive there. Those who you lead will need to see the vision and experience your tenacity in order to buy into the team's goals and objectives. Many books have been written on leading others as it is certainly an area that you will need to master on your leadership journey. First, it all begins with you. You must lead yourself well so you can lead others well and teach them the same habits.

Why do we need great leaders now? We need great leaders now more than ever to shine the light on who we are meant to be and what we are called to do. In John 9:5 NIV, Jesus says, "While I am in the world, I am the light of the world." We revere great leaders like Gandhi, Martin Luther King, Jr., Nelson Mandela, Margaret Thatcher, and Stacey Abrams because they have tapped into their God-given potential which is their true power in order to impact and change humanity for the better and for lifetimes to come. Those in the shadows who were not seen, they shone their light and in turn improved the consciousness of the global human family. If you have a calling to lead you must lead and use your God-given power for good. We all have it. We came to this Earth school not merely to exist but to share our talents with the world.

# Living My Truth By Leading Myself

My earliest memory of leading myself comes from my childhood memories of bottlefeeding my six-month old sister with my left hand and doing my homework with my right. I recall my mother pursuing her college degree while having five daughters under the age of nine. I grew up with a high level of expectation to assume responsibility for my siblings and to lead the way as the first daughter. I do not recall feeling any resentment about these seemingly high expectations for a child because frankly I enjoyed being the "boss," and it came with a generous portion of praise and accolades from my parents. Being raised by two educators, the name of the game in my household was 'excellence.' I was expected to be a high achiever, and so naturally, my decision to pursue medicine as a career was a point of pride for my parents. I was inherently self-motivated, was sent to the best private schools in Europe, and received a lot of academic coaching in the home as well.

Our home was an extension of the classroom. My parents were avid readers, so we had the latest versions of encyclopedias to pursue our studies. In this environment, I grew up believing that I could have it all. With belief in myself, I knew if I pursued anything with sufficient fervor and perseverance I could achieve it. My mother's courage to go back to school after having five children forever left an impression on me that nothing was impossible as long as I believed in it, desired it, and focused on it.

My parents' expectation of nothing but excellence fostered my perfectionist personality that has served me well in my professional pursuits. Although I immigrated to the United States at the age of fifteen solo, without the rest of my family, I felt ready to embark upon the journey of becoming the first doctor in my family. My parents had provided a solid educational foundation both outside and within the home, and they equipped me with the right mindset to succeed. My dream to come to America, be the immigrant who became a doctor, would come to fruition.

I recall an experience in one of my residency programs where I was summoned to speak to a supervisor for a complaint that had been rendered against me. The complaint was "You are too confident." I was dumbfounded that a 'non-confident' physician would be preferred. Was this because I was female, African-American, or both? I truly wondered in that order. I had been in the workforce for three years before attending medical school and six years in postgraduate training prior to this complaint. Thus far, I had not been perceived as an arrogant individual in my professional evaluations. Who could be threatened by my confidence? How many other ways could I interpret confidence? My baseline is confidence, humility and self-assuredness. In my DNA is written Philippians 4:13 NIV: "I can do all this through him who gives me strength." Today I unapologetically walk away from any individual or entity that tells me that I can't have it all. This mindset is what has brought me to where I am today: owning my voice, accepting my power, and choosing to use it to empower millions more.

I can say that my journey as a physician is an area where I had to lead myself—but I was lucky to have good counsel from my mentors. In all areas of my life, in particular my professional life, I strived for excellence, I did not do so merely for personal or financial gain but because I truly believed that the power of my creator resided in me and it was my duty to tap into it; I believed in the biblical saying that "your gifts will make room for you." So I ventured in all my deeds to identify what my gift is because not only will it bring me joy but it would also bless others. Excellence, to me, never meant having all the clinical answers, but rather experiencing moments of being present with my patients, serving with humility and compassion to the extent that they knew I was one with them in our shared human experience. This sense of presence between clinicians and their patients is often missing in modern day medicine with all its demands to meet ever burgeoning measures and milestones, but it is for that very reason that our patients seek solace in our counsel.

## Five Mantras

1. Your dream is yours and you alone are responsible for seeing it to fruition.

2.  A great leader knows that there is no such thing as failures; merely challenges or stumbling blocks, which are a part of the journey of leadership.

3.  Courage means having the willingness to go through trials and tribulations and allowing them to shape you into who you were meant to be.

4.  You cannot take your team to a destination where you personally have not gone or are willing to go.

5.  We came to this Earth School not merely to exist but to share our talents with the world.

# What is the next best step for making the transition into living your truth?

Identify your gifts and talents that you would love to share with humanity.

# CHAPTER 4

# No Glass Ceiling: If there are footprints on the moon, is the sky the limit?

*The problem with gender is that it prescribes how we should be rather than recognizing how we are.*

—Chimamanda Ngozi Adichie

Living your truth allows you to fulfill your potential. You see no limits. There are no limits. You can defy all the odds. You can go as far as you want to go. You can pursue your dreams with full abandonment and with no restrictions placed on you except the one you place on yourself.

What does 'no glass ceilings' mean? It means that you must believe in yourself and not accept any limitations placed upon you. It means you focus only on the possibilities and not on your circumstances or anything else that can hold you back. Possibilities keep your mindset in the posture of receiving, in contradiction to the mindset of lack. Focus on what is the out-come and live in the acceptance that the manifestation of the vision has already occurred. A limitless individual is a lifelong learner, one who is not intimidated by potential roadblocks along the journey of success. Roadblocks are only viewed as stepping-stones, necessary challenges that must be overcome to realize the wish and see the dream fulfilled. Being limitless is a yearning for that which all souls desire: freedom.

How do we prepare for the challenges that certainly will occur? Do not be afraid of challenges for they are part of the process and will only serve to sharpen and grow you. Accept challenges as battles to overcome in order to inherit the spoils of the war. Continue to raise the bar, improve your standards to improve your life. Ask yourself daily the following: How can I improve my standards to improve my circumstance? Be still and listen and the answers will surely come. You will find it helpful to work with an accountability partner that will encourage you, motivate you, push you, and support you to maintain the goals that you have set for yourself. In health and in my professional life, I sought accountability partners to help me reach my goals; whether I was trying to finish a tough semester in med school, achieve and maintain a fitness goal, or when I started to write this book. I sought dependable individuals to partner with and we supported each other till the very end of the project. Do what seems hard immediate-ly, right now; for procrastination will not make the challenge disappear or be less daunting. The human spirit is extremely resilient such that the more you challenge yourself, the more you grow and accomplish; and eventually you will look back and wonder why you ever had any fears. One of my favorite quotes from Nelson Mandela reads: "It seems impossible until it is done." This to me captures how to be limitless: Remain unstoppable until what seems impossible is done.

How to stay inspired and motivated? Keep your why, your purpose, your reason for existence before you at all times because it is only you and you alone who is responsible for keeping yourself motivated. Remember that your vision and your dreams were given to you. Read daily affirmations and journal daily about aspects of your life for which you are grateful. Gratitude brings miracles. I truly believe this. Try it. Remember that others may participate on your journey to being limitless for specific periods of time, however the only one to rely on is you. One of my favorite mantras is: If it's meant to be, then it's up to me. Stay motivated by being extremely selective about that which you bring into your awareness. Read, watch, listen, expose yourself only to subjects that inspire and support you to become the better version of yourself. Staying motivated and keeping yourself inspired therefore becomes a daily habit.

Become the expert. It is necessary to continue to find challenges that will keep you growing, relevant and ultimately expand your sphere of influence. Never settle on your past accomplishments, but rather stay current in your field of expertise and avoid becoming outdated at all costs. Continue reading on to the next chapter for further discussion on self-mastery. When you discover that which brings you joy; you would then want to figure out a way to make a living doing it. Being passionate about what you do such that it does not feel laborious will truly become one of the greatest accomplishments of your life, and the secret to a joyous life.

How to deal with challenges? Challenges are opportunities for growth and must be seen that way to stay encouraged while your goals and objectives unfold. Challenges may draw us closer to our faith because we start to recognize how resilient we are becoming in the face of obstacles. I am often amazed at the obstacles I have overcome in my life journey which on the onset always seemed impossible and daunting to surmount. When you have faith in the greater power within you, you believe in that which is unseen as seen; until that which is not seen becomes seen. Having faith is vital as it will keep you going and sustain you during the many tough situations that lie ahead. Making the assumption that you already have in possession that which you desire will enable you to see every obstacle in the journey as necessary toward accomplishing your chief goals. Challenges are merely opportunities to master complex situations which need to be solved as the pieces of any puzzle that must come together. The answers may not always come swiftly but you must trust and believe that the solutions are all within you. He who has the problem also has the solution.

# Living to Break All Glass Ceilings

There were several circumstances in my professional career where I have been underestimated. These circumstances only served to fuel my passion for accomplishing my dreams. My approach to these circumstances has always been one of bewilderment that anyone could see less for me than I could see for myself followed by inner peace and self-assuredness that I knew I could accomplish any goal that I set for myself. All credit to my parents for raising a very confident child and their approach of raising the bar of achievement early on in my upbringing whilst giving me the tools and support I needed to be successful. Certainly their parenting style played a large role in creating a self-confident child and my enhanced self-awareness as an adult.

A similar example that bewildered me the most was the situation of a premedical advisor not believing that I should go to medical school. In my gut I knew that was not true. I knew my desire to become a physician was for me, I knew the world was waiting for me to bring this gift. When it came to future interactions with this particular advisor, I decided it was best to keep my hopes and dreams to myself and only communicate what was absolutely necessary. The dream was not given to her, it was given to me. I was very disappointed that I did not have the support of my assigned premedical advisor at that particular junction in my personal development. However, I was by no means deflated. I understand now that sometimes those you confide in will try to protect you from what they feel may be painful experiences for you. It is up to us to decide if those potential 'failures' and painful experiences are worth it. I am here to tell you that it was all worth it; I would not change a thing. All have made me better, stronger, and more resilient in all areas of my life. After graduating from college, I decided to pursue my master's degree in public health because I believed that it would assure my entrance into medical school and at the time, I desired someday to work with an international health organization as both a clinician advisor and a public health specialist.

While attending my master's program, I worked for a research consulting firm and my boss at the time did not believe I should go to medical school right away; he suggested working for him for two years or more, furthering my work experience with his firm. and then applying to medical school.

No individual could deter me from the belief that I would become a physician. No matter how tough a semester I was having or the fact that I had immigrated alone without my family. I never did ask those individuals why they thought I would not make a good fit or that I needed to wait. I had good grades, good enough MCAT (medical college admission test) scores, strong letters of recommendation, and had held several jobs while carrying a full load of credits per semester, as well as notable internships. In the case of my boss, he was shocked when six months later, I presented to him my admissions letter to a top medical school in the country: Rutgers! Believe it or not, he claimed credit for my acceptance to medical school and boldly affirmed that "*We* did it." Even though he did not wish it for me, and I did not seek any professional assistance from him through the process. I am eternally grateful for the opportunity he provided and the promotions I received—from research assistant to research associate, during my tenure at the firm. These promotions likely propelled my acceptance into medical school.

Break through limiting beliefs and believe in yourself more than anyone else. I sought motivation not from outside of myself but from within, and I set my standards as high as I could imagine in order to witness the manifestation of my dreams. According to Neville Goddard, author of *The Power of Awareness*, one must yield completely to the assumption of having or becoming that which one desires in order to experience it. In other words, he says: One must have loyalty to the unseen reality, which is, unshakeable faith; and because I had this level of faith and believe in my God-given potential, I could see in myself what no other person could.

# Five Mantras

1. Being limitless means believing that only the manifestation of the vision is acceptable to you and nothing else.

2. Do what seems hard and the rest will fall into place and become easier.

3. Stay motivated by being extremely selective about that which you bring into your awareness.

4. Never settle on your past accomplishments, but rather stay current in your field of expertise and avoid at all costs becoming outdated.

5. Challenges or opportunities for growth and must be seen as such in order to remain encouraged while your goals and objectives unfold.

## What is the next best step for making the transition into living your truth?

Leaders are readers. Read or listen to at least one to two books per month in the area of personal development.

# CHAPTER 5

# Personal Growth and Development: What does success look like for you?

*The only person you are destined to become
is the person you decide to be.*

**—Ralph Waldo Emerson**

This is your time to develop the content of your skill that will lead to lifelong impact. How will you know unless you give yourself a chance? Now you begin the journey of self-mastery. The road may be rough and laced with uncertainties but the results are sure to reveal the diamond within you.

Why self-mastery? It is important to distinguish yourself as an expert in your field. You've probably heard the saying that "School is never out for the pro," which means the journey to mastery is never over. Self-mastery is necessary for your growth and development because it is only when we know ourselves that we can begin to love ourselves for who we are and ponder if we need to change the habits that no longer serve us. Self-mastery starts with paying attention to what you are thinking about. Does what you are thinking about serve your greater good? Pay attention without judgment and decide if what you are thinking about is what your soul knows about you.

What are you good at? Identify your gift by deciding what brings you joy. What brings you joy is an indicator of how you could continue to develop yourself and grow your skills. When you focus on self-mastery, you will also begin to identify your gifts. It is your gifts that will open doors for you. You were endowed with a special gift by your Creator that you were meant to share with the world. You came to this Earth School to do something meaningful and impactful. Have you discovered what it is yet? Discover it, develop it, share it with the world, and you will have truly lived a successful life.

What do you need to work on to accomplish your goals? As you walk the journey of self-mastery you will mostly identify areas that you need to develop. This is a necessary step as you begin to hone your skills. For there is no such thing as being perfect, however, you can certainly become a master in your art. There will *always* be something more to learn, to improve on; and this is good and so intended because as human beings we are called to continuously increase and expand in our awareness. When you stop growing, you die; your art dies;

your call to greatness dies. Do not let it die. Keep the flame burning by continuing to improve yourself. In whatever areas you identify as a weakness, it will soon become a strength as long as you work on it, practice it and eventually master it.

Where are your opportunities for growth? If you think about it, there are so many areas you can find opportunities for growth. First identify the areas in which you desire to grow. Then seek mentorship in those areas. Mentorship is vital to success because there is always someone ahead of you who can pave the way for you or support you with developing your skills. It is important to seek mentorship in any area in which you choose to grow. The mentor-mentee relationship is a sacred one and it should not be taken advantage of. Always ask permission for the time that has been given to you freely; show your gratitude by being prepared and respecting that time. Also seek ways in which you can serve your mentor as it should be a mutually advantageous experience. Remember to also take advantage of the vast amount of resources available online including joining or following on social media the organizations and/or interest groups that may be involved in your area of interest. What conferences can you attend to learn more about your field? What are the books that your mentor reads and that you should be reading too? There is no end to opportunities for growth. Remember, it can be beneficial to have more than one mentor depending on their availability or if there are multiple areas you are developing at the same time.

You must continue to challenge and stretch yourself to remain relevant in your field of expertise.

What could threaten your success? Fears, self-doubts, and indecisiveness could threaten your success. Procrastination is based on the fear of not being perfect and fear of being judged negatively—and that can paralyze your success as well. Procrastination is the Achilles' heel of the one who is a perfectionist. Self-doubt may stem from lack of confidence, resources, low self-esteem, or past negative experiences. These all lead to negative programming or negative thinking of oneself that leads to inaction and ultimately inertia. It is important to realize that there is no failure in the journey of personal growth and development; there is only learning. When we embody negative experiences or negative emotions on this journey as failure, we miss an opportunity to grow in that very same area. You cannot be a failure but you can miss the opportunity to deliver your unique gifts to the world, which was the only reason you came. It was to deliver your light and make the world a brighter place. Imagine if all of humanity brought their light. Add your flicker and let your light shine.

## Living the Journey of Personal Growth

Dilapidated rural clinics and ill-equipped city hospitals!

Village health workers with meager or no medical supplies!

My baby sister, unconscious with a high fever!

As a young girl, these were some of my most striking memories. I recall feeling that my sister might die with febrile convulsions and with no treatment in sight; and crying with joy when she recovered, knowing that not everyone in our rural village in Imo State, Nigeria, where we visited infrequently, was this lucky. Women and children seemed to be the population hardest hit by poor health conditions. Under the scorching heat of the sun, they would wait patiently outside the health center for medical attention and for the only physician for several kilometers. I remember experiencing severe dysentery that could have been avoided had there been basic public health services such as clean water and proper sanitation. When my family relocated to Vienna, Austria, we had better access to healthcare, including those house calls from our family physician, during which the seeds for a passionate career were sewn and my aspirations for becoming a healer were born.

Given my memories in childhood of abject poverty and human suffering, I felt an indelible responsibility and a calling throughout my higher education to become the best version of myself in all my endeavors. My memories served me well, and freed me from wanting permission from any soul to pursue my calling to the highest level possible. My thought and belief has always been that investing in my skills and mindset would become my superpower and allow me to give back to all communities that I would be privileged to serve.

## Five Mantras

1. Self-mastery begins with paying attention to what you were thinking about.

2. You were endowed with a special gift by your Creator that you were meant to share with the world.

3. There is no such thing as being perfect; however, you can become a master in your art.

4. The human spirit is limitless and knows no boundaries.

5. There is no failure in the journey of personal growth and development, only learning. The only failure is quitting.

## What is the next best step for making the transition into living your truth?

Perform your own analysis of your personal strengths, weaknesses, opportunities, and threats to begin to identify areas for growth.

# CHAPTER 6

# Freedom: Are you thinking for yourself?

*Everything that is really great and inspiring is created by the individual who can labor in freedom.*

**—Albert Einstein**

Freedom to come. Freedom to go. Freedom to set your own agenda. Freedom is the oxygen of the spirit. You are now the master of your fate, the captain of your ship. You are finally standing up for yourself. You have chosen to make your life beautiful and meaningful.

Why freedom? This would be akin to saying, "Why breathe?" All souls desire freedom because as individuals we are inherently born limitless with a desire to expand in our consciousness, awareness, and possibilities. If you believe in yourself, there is no limit to what you can be, do, or achieve. Freedom of choice, thought, and time allows you to create and imagine that all things are indeed achievable. The most valuable thing we possess is our freedom and this comes in the form of time for yourself for self-development and self-expression. When we trade our time for money we diminish our opportunity to become the best version of ourselves. Trading time for money making never brings true freedom. Hence, we focus on our gifts which will always make room for us; room to be free.

What is the value of freedom? Nelson Mandela once said, "For to be free is not merely to cast off one's chains, but to live in a way that respects and enhances the freedom of others." Being free to set and master your own course empowers you to do the same for others. All souls desire freedom and all souls desire to see their dreams manifest. The problem is that as individuals we are so often stuck in fear, doubt, and indecisiveness. Political freedom fighter Aung San Suu Kyi once said that "the only real prison is fear and the only real freedom is freedom from fear." I cannot think of a more perfect quote to describe the value of freedom.

What is not freedom? Regardless of what role you have in the workforce, be it the chairman or the janitor, if you are being told what to wear, when to clock in, when to clock out, what to do, what to say or when to take vacation, then you are not free—especially if you do not agree with what you are being told. If your core values or vision are not in alignment with that of your employer then you are not free. If it feels dreadful to rise up every morning to earn a living because your spirit is simply not joyful, then you are not free. The human spirit is limitless and thus yearns for growth and expansion. Therefore, any experience in life that gives you the feeling of freedom to tap into your creative genius is setting you on your path to freedom.

How do you earn freedom? The great Buddha once said, "No one outside ourselves can rule us inwardly; when we know this we become free." I find this extremely liberating because it tells me that I am the one in control if I believe it." Remember that you own your thoughts and that it is your thoughts alone that create your future. When you accept this, you now choose carefully the thoughts that you are affirming for yourself. You now choose the thoughts that give you courage and liberate you on your journey to becoming free and fearless. So what will you choose today to think about your potential? Choose wisely because you are creating the next version of you.

On the freedom journey, you will stumble, you will make mistakes and you will experience fears and doubts. However, nothing worth having comes easy and when you realize that you can be, do, have anything that you aim for, you do it boldly. Freedom is all inclusive, so it will come with successes and perceived failures. As Mahatma Ghandi once said, "Freedom is not worth having if it does not include freedom to make mistakes." Within your failures, lies your successes, and it is through the experience of adversity that you will shape your character. Courage is not the absence of fear; but it is the presence of fear with faith and determination. Stay encouraged, and true freedom is soon to follow.

# Living for Freedom

The writing of this book coincides at a time in my life where I am experiencing the most personal and professional freedom. It took this moment of working for myself, launching into the world of entrepreneurship, and building my own practice before I could experience yet another form of freedom: the writing of this book as a means to amplify my voice beyond the four walls of the patient's exam room. I had to let go of all the elements of living life in a manner that was traditional and 'expected' of a physician in order to experience the true calling of the healer within.

I am finally chasing my passion, not money nor title, and feeling liberated in doing so. This sense of liberation is akin to an artist who is free to create and develop his work of art. I am feeling free to allow my creativity to flow, to let the music of my soul sing. Knowing what I know about the Law of Attraction leads me to believe that the vibration of my energy is at a level that matches the energy of thought and brings the energy of my desire into my reality. Writing brings me joy and brought me freedom.

# Five Mantras

1. The most valuable thing we possess is our freedom and this comes in the form of time for yourself for self-development and self-expression.

2. All souls desire freedom and all souls desire to see their dreams manifest.

3. If it feels dreadful to rise up every morning to earn a living because your spirit is not joyful, then you are not free.

4. No one can control you inwardly, and if you believe this, you control your destiny.

5. Within your failures lie your successes and it is through the experience of adversity that you will shape your character.

# What is the next best step for making the transition into living your truth?

Chase your passions—not money—to find true freedom. Write down all that drives you and brings you joy to find your freedom.

# CHAPTER 7

# Flexibility: Are you wise enough to remain flexible?

*In this moment, there's infinite possibility, and this is the agility that gives me flexibility to overcome my situation when my situation's killing me.*

—Curtis Tyrone Jones

When you are flexible, you are giving yourself a chance to be better, a chance to fail forward to success. You can fully embrace your own creativity and different ways of getting the job done. Being flexible is an important attribute for discovering your unique strengths and talents.

A Reward? Yes. Flexibility is one of the best rewards of living your truth. It should be truly embraced and relished. For so long you have been waiting for this moment. A chance to breathe again. A chance to think again for yourself. A chance to be free. A chance to soar. A chance to discover what you're really made of. A chance to control your own destiny.

What I've truly enjoyed the most about being my own boss is the freedom to schedule my priorities and not prioritize my schedule. The great Lao Tzu once said: "A man is born gentle and weak. At death he is hard and stiff. Green plants are tender and filled with sap. At death, they are withered and dry. Therefore, the stiff and unbending is the disciple of death, and the gentle and yielding is the disciple of life."

Why is it important to be flexible? Well, change is a constant. Therefore, with more flexibility in your life, you're able to adapt to constant change because it is a necessity to achieving your goals. And because you're able to adapt, you're able to be more stable. Lose flexibility and you lose stability. Flexibility is also intrinsic with being adaptable which leads to more opportunities for growth. More opportunities for growth sets you up for success in changing times; you're able to adjust to the unexpected and to the vicissitudes of life. Hence, being flexible is vital to your evolution and to becoming the better version of yourself.

Leading people well demands flexibility. Great leaders adhere to their core values and principles but are always flexible in their approach to their mission. This is because they know that being flexible is at the core of expansion and building a great team of like-minded leaders. To lead others also requires a varying degree of strategies that will accommodate different levels of ability and talent. Erik Pevernagie, the Belgian artist, once said, "When the whole world is entrenched in the bunker of physical and often emotional isolation, only flexibility and ingenuity can revive us to remain grounded and imbibe the bolstering sunlight piercing through the canvas of chaos." Without flexibility our mind perishes in a world of its own that no longer exists because we failed to adapt to change.

Creative people are flexible. When you are flexible, you have more room to be creative. You experience the palpable stillness of your surroundings that allows the mind to flow more naturally, more freely and bring forth its creative genius. Such an attribute means you're able to constantly reinvent yourself to meet the demands of a growing and changing world. Anton St. Maarten once said, "Blessed are the flexible, for change is inevitable. To fulfill our true destiny as spiritual beings we must trust in our divine power to adapt." I find this quite comforting because it reassures us not to be afraid of change, but rather to embrace it as part of our soul's journey.

Flexibility is a bridge to greatness. It goes without saying then that arriving at your destiny will require an appreciable amount of patience, perseverance and flexibility. Your bridge to greatness will encompass not only fortitude but also mental flexibility coupled with perhaps an unquantifiable dose of resilience. If you remain flexible, you will be able to maneuver through the various obstacles that will present as roadblocks on your course. However, stand in belief for all that you desire and you will surely thrive and bridge all your adversities. In this life, strive to maintain a mindset of flexibility which will expose you to infinite growth possibilities, that will develop you and unleash the power within you to be a force for good.

## Living and Yearning for Flexibility

The core of my being yearns for freedom to express all the talents endowed upon me by my Creator and the flexibility to mold into form my experiences according to my own imagination. Given my passion for learning and travel, I eventually realized that I thrived best both physically and psychologically in settings that allowed my creative thoughts to flow and find their ultimate expression in the written word. I believe that all humans desire this but few have the opportunity to explore or entertain this inherent gift of life.

As an entrepreneur, having more flexibility has allowed me to become better in so many areas of my life. Most importantly, I've been able to spend more quality time with my family, more supportive time with ailing family members, more time to produce creatively, more time to develop my practice, more time to develop my business coaching program for building women leaders in the direct sales self-care and skin care industry, and finally, more time for personal development and self-care. It has been a long road to getting back to listening to the silent whisper within me that has been trying to direct me toward my greater good. Finally putting myself first, by deciding to leave the four walls of medicine and envision the possibility of delivering health and wellness in a more sustainable way for both doctor and patient, is allowing me to tap into the power within me (and that resides within all of us) to make it a reality.

## Five Mantras

1. Having more flexibility in your life is one of the best rewards of living your truth.

2. With more flexibility in your life, you're able to adapt to constant change.

3. Being flexible is vital to your evolution to becoming the person you were meant to be.

4. Without flexibility, our mind perishes in a world of its own that no longer exists because we failed to adapt to change.

5. Your bridge to greatness will encompass fortitude, mental flexibility, and resilience.

## What is the next best step for making the transition into living your truth?

Embrace flexibility in all areas of your life as long as it does not compromise your core values.

# CHAPTER 8

# Be Limitless: Are you ready for the adventure of your lifetime?

*Just like moons and like suns, with the certainty of tides, just like hopes springing high, still I rise.*

—Maya Angelou

You have probably heard the saying that there is no comfort in the comfort zone. All adventures into new territories can wreak havoc on your nerves; however, new territories means no limits to what you can achieve. You are free to explore and truly discover your potential. Because you are on a new adventure, your past never has to limit your future. There is greatness within you, remember that.

Removing self-limiting beliefs is the first step toward becoming limitless, and ultimately becoming who we were called to be. These are beliefs we hold about ourselves that make us feel less than who we really are. These are beliefs that make us feel small, insignificant and make us want to hide. These are beliefs that keep us "safe" from feeling what we perceive as the disdain of others' opinions. These are beliefs ascribed to us by people, circumstances or experiences from our past lives that we falsely adopted as part of our identity.

Becoming fearless is necessary. When you are fearless, you become limitless. When your vision is clear, you will not allow any person or circumstance to stand in your way. Everyone in your path is here to live their journey. Your resolve should only be to work on yourself, to change yourself and not to change anyone else or anyone's impression of who you are. When you focus on yourself, you focus on what really matters. If it instills fear in you, you must conquer it. During WWII as General of the U.S. Army, Teddy Roosevelt, is famous for saying, "The only thing to fear is fear itself."

Believing in yourself means believing in the power of your Creator, that resides within you. If you truly believed that there was such power within you, how would you show up for yourself, your family and your life circumstances? Would your goals and aspirations take on a different meaning? Would your self-limiting thoughts become less debilitating to your goals and dreams? Believing in yourself is closely tied into the idea of removing self-limiting beliefs because as you get rid of self-limiting beliefs, you are becoming a true believer…of you.

Imperfection is a part of human existence. There will always be imperfection in the human form. According to the teachings of Neville Goddard, God became man so that man may become God. We are created in His image and thus within us there is intrinsic greatness. The key is to embrace this greatness, this power that lies within us. However, throughout the course of our lives, we are faced with challenges and circumstances beyond our control that break our spirit and leave us feeling helpless. Our suffering is not meant to be erased but to be appreciated and utilized as a point of reference from who we are now to who we are meant to become. Without imperfection, there is no contrast. Contrast is necessary to help identify what we don't want, so that by knowing what we don't want, we begin to understand what we do want.

Do not be consumed by others' opinion of you. This is a problem for so many and it can leave one extremely paralyzed. You want to obliterate immediately what people think of you from your consciousness. What is for you is meant for you. Your desires are your desires. Your dreams are your dreams. Michael Gelb once said, "By stretching yourself beyond your perceived level of confidence you accelerate your development of competence."

# Living Limitless

There is an earning potential cap in medicine and as a primary care female physician I had approached it. The marketplace places a greater monetary value on the skills of specialists compared to the skills of primary care physicians. As I worked harder and longer hours, I saw my earning potential essentially plateau. The salary cap was a smaller concern in comparison with the gap between my core values and where my career had gone. The corporate core values were impressive on paper, but in practice were not in alignment with my own. It was at this junction in my career that I decided the time had come for me to be my own boss and discover my hidden potential.

On this journey I discovered that there were other physicians out there just like me, who did not quite fit into the walls of medicine and were looking for ways to use their skills and give value in a manner that was reflective of their purpose, passion and core values. At the same time, I had been exploring the direct sales industry and noticed that I was making an impact in the arena of leadership. In seven short months from joining Mary Kay Cosmetics, I had become a sales director. Over the following two years I would develop two other leaders and grow my team to more than 100 women. I discovered that there was no limit in the earning potential in direct sales and I would be compensated for my efforts. The additional income would not only fund my health and wellness practice but would allow me to pursue other interests, such as completing this manuscript and pursuing other philanthropic projects.

I discovered that my skills in leadership as a physician were transferable to my Mary Kay skin care business. I was encouraging other women, coaching them to be their best selves, and giving them tools to do so, just as I was doing as a doctor. The company's philosophy of God first, family second, and career third was evident in the lives of the leaders that mentored me and it was in alignment with my own core values. In medicine, my desire was to build a practice that would encompass my core values and give me the freedom and flexibility to explore other interests, such as writing this book, traveling the world, exploring medical missions and spending much needed time with my family. In the arena of my skin care business, I discovered tremendous joy in coaching and inspiring women to become leaders of their own destiny. This inspired me to develop a coaching program that would do just that: a program that would take them through a mindset change, from doubt to courage to confidence, such that they can have more opportunities to live a life of purpose. I love for women to have more choices, because it is only when we have more choices that we can become truly limitless.

The version of medicine I had been practicing all this time was limiting my truest potential because of the time constraints with patients, the significant staff shortages, the massive documentation requirements, and the seismic differences between the unspoken corporate core values and my own. I knew that there had to be a better way, and after eighteen years of being a physician, I finally found the courage to begin to create to my own private practice with a focus on health and wellness. As I came to this realization and decided to walk away from being an employed physician, I discovered that other areas of my life were improving as well. I had finally given myself the permission to design a practice that would allow me to show up in the most authentic version of myself, placing what mattered the most to me first: faith, family, career. I experienced this way of living as an adult from being a member of the salesforce of Mary Kay Inc.

In the skin care industry, my desire is to build up the confidence of women and develop leaders who will go forth to inspire millions more to believe in themselves and their dreams and to never accept any limitations on their capacity. With the growth of my team, the priceless training and the mentorship of phenomenal leaders the company such as my Senior National Sales Director (SNSD) Elizabeth Muna, Emerti NSD Joanne Barnes, NSD Temi Odeyale, NSD Pam Higgs, and EESNSD, Dr. Gloria Mayfield Banks, my vision to mentor and inspire women globally has come to fruition. In May 2021, I was accepted into Mary Kay's Global Development Leadership Program which meant I could also expand my business internationally to Canada. It was definitely an act of faith to transition from my corporate medical position to working from home to spend quality time with myself and my family, to begin to create the practice of my imagination, and to embrace global entrepreneurship. I finally found the courage to follow my inner truth and only align my spirit with situations that were true to my core values, would bring me joy, allow me to be limitless and become an expression of the best version of myself in all areas of my life, starting with my faith, my family and then my career.

# Five Mantras

1. Limiting beliefs are lies ascribed to us by people and circumstances or experiences from our past lives that we falsely adopted as part of our identity.

2. Your resolve should be to change yourself and not to change anyone else or their impression of who you are. They will know you by your deeds.

3. Believing in yourself means believing in the power of your Creator that resides within you.

4. Contrast in our lives is necessary to help identify what we don't want; so by knowing what we don't want we will begin to understand what we do want on the journey of life.

5. Do not let the opinions of others paralyze you.

# What is the next best step for making the transition into living your truth?

What are the limiting beliefs that you hold about yourself and how can you begin to let go of them today?

# CHAPTER 9

# Legacy: How will they remember you?

*It always seems impossible until it is done.*

—Nelson Mandela

What difference did you make while you were here on the Earth School? How many hearts did you touch? Now is the time to set the stage to leave your legacy. Make your presence felt now on the heartbeat of humanity. It is not the years of life lived that counts but the impact of your presence that matters.

Why does legacy matter? I believe that every soul on this planet came here with a purpose. There is a gift buried deep within each and every one of us that we were meant to deliver when we arrived at this Earth school. The sooner we can discover that gift, embrace it, harness it, the sooner we will be living the purpose-driven life that our soul yearns for and that we were meant to live. When we embody a purpose-driven life, when we truly accomplish this, we become the best version of ourselves and that is what the world needs. Hence, the token greatness that lies within each of us then manifests and becomes the legacy that we leave behind.

How does one leave a legacy? One leaves a legacy through self-love, belief in oneself, identifying one's gift, and harnessing the creative power that lies within oneself to bring forth that gift and share it with the world. You leave a legacy by believing that all things—good and bad—are working for your greater good and only exist to show you contrast. Without contrast you wouldn't know what you want or don't want. So appreciate the contrast and see them for what they truly are; tools to sharpen you on your legacy journey. You will then consequently let go of your fears, doubts and limiting beliefs. You leave a legacy by accepting that no matter the lack of evidence of the manifestation of the wish fulfilled, you nonetheless believe in yourself and the vision, and you follow through with inspired action, for it will all surely manifest. The inherent belief in oneself is so vital as it will carry through all the tough and certainly the trying times.

On the road to creating your legacy, you will begin by assuming you are now, that which you desire to become. In life, you only become who you are and not who you want to be. As a man thinketh, so is he. This is so true and it must be analyzed to be fully understood. So who are you being now? How do you think of yourself now? What are you assuming of yourself now? Is what you assume now who you are? If not, change it right now. You must impress on your subconscious mind now, the legacy for which you wish to be known for. How will they know your good works? How would it feel right now if you were already that person who you desire to be? How would it feel right now if your legacy has already manifested. When you impress these feelings onto your subconscious mind, they will manifest because your subconscious mind is not subjective. Your subconscious mind is objective and whatever you believe as truth is what you will see in your reality. You are truly the creator of your own reality and you can be anything you want to be through the power of your own thoughts. So think wisely, for as a man thinketh, so is he.

What did you accomplish? Now that you know that you are the creator of your own thoughts, and that you cannot fail unless you do nothing, what inspired action will you take? Only consider your next best step. This is one way to prevent from feeling the overwhelm of any big dream. Take the next best step and then the next and you will soon witness your very own creation materialize. The time we have on this Earth School is so precious and so fleeting that so many go to their graves with the dreams buried within them. Let this not be the story of your legacy, that you came and you did nothing with your gifts and talents. We all have them. It is up to you to discover it, polish it, share it and it will bring you all the abundance of life that you are seeking. Remember that your gifts will always make room for you. Follow your passion, purpose, calling and the money will follow you. Take inspired action and let your dreams be your inspiration.

There is no such thing as failure. Once you accept this as fact, you will never give up on your dreams. Henceforth, whatever you perceive as failure, see it instead as learning or insight into one more way *not* to do something. Imagine if Thomas Edison had given up on the light bulb or if Alexander Graham Bell had given up on the telephone. They had dreams to impact civilization and they never stopped until they did. Imagine if Martin Luther King, Jr., gave up on his dream. What would the state of civil rights be today? Imagine if Nelson Mandela gave up his calling for justice for South Africans and all oppressed peoples of the world? Would generations not linger in darkness? Remember that your dreams were meant for you. Your dreams were meant for humanity and when you deliver on the promise, you deliver yourself from bondage and millions more that you may never know. That is the meaning of true legacy. Freedom for you, liberty for generations. Remember you were created in His image, therefore you are perfect in your imperfection. Creation is complete and so all that you desire has already been created and waiting for you to receive it. The universe awaits your legacy. Now is your time to deliver.

# Living for the Legacy

As a frontline physician during the pandemic of 2020, I saw my life and that of millions more globally change drastically. After approximately one year in that position, several familial challenges made it necessary to work from home. I did not know until I had left the position the indelible impact I had made on the hearts of so many. My daily goal at the position was to show up as my most authentic self and to work with my staff and patients to get through the myriad challenges of life and work during a global pandemic.

In my role as director with Mary Kay Inc, I try to also partner with the women that I have the privilege to mentor and in which I see myself as a servant leader. When I approached a few of my team members for feedback on the impact of my leadership on their progress, I was simply humbled by the accolades that I received. I share this here simply to illustrate that leading with a heart that is committed to the betterment of others and helping them achieve their goals is extremely rewarding.

# Five Mantras

1. When we embody a purpose-driven life we become the best version of ourselves and that is what the world needs.

2. Believe in yourself and your vision and follow through to see it fulfilled.

3.  Your subconscious mind is objective and whatever you believe as truth is what you will see in your reality

4.  Follow your passion, purpose, calling and the money will always follow you.

5.  Your dreams were meant to be expressed by you for the benefit of mankind.

# What is the next best step for making the transition into living your truth?

Write down all that you are proficient in and can master with ease.

# CHAPTER 10

# Follow Your Soul's Purpose: What is your calling?

*I have brought you glory on earth by finishing
the work you gave me to do.*

—John 17:4 NIV

Are you ready to experience true joy and happiness? You are free and flexible to put your heart, mind, body, and soul into everything you do. This act alone, if persevered upon, will surely lead to success. Though the intellect may resist, your soul always knows when it is time to close a chapter and begin another. Live in your truth to satisfy your soul. It takes courage but you are worth it.

You must follow your soul's purpose in order to become the truest version of yourself. You are a human body in a soul and not a soul in a body. Your soul came to a school called Earth through you, to have a human experience. That soul has a purpose that you were meant to identify and fulfill. The sooner you can identify that purpose and begin to live it, the sooner you will feel that your life's journey has been a success; the sooner you will feel that you have fulfilled the calling of your soul.

Why follow your soul's purpose? You must follow your soul's purpose to experience the peace which surpasses all understanding; to experience the joy of today. You must follow your soul's purpose to live your best human life now. Your soul loves every part of who you truly are, because who you truly are is who you were authentically created to become; and that version of you lives in your imagination and in the vision you have always had for your life. It is up to you to identify who you are authentically and give yourself permission to become it and live in that truth today. If every human were to follow their soul's purpose, which is the truest calling to greatness, the world would be a much better place with less competition, strife and anguish.

When should you follow? Is tomorrow promised? Every day we live is another day of grace given to us. You never quit searching for your soul's purpose. Your soul lies patiently waiting for you to begin your journey to personal fulfillment. That journey was not only meant for you, but for all who see you. The message here is to be the light of the world. Follow the soul, your light so you can be free. Be the light so others can see and be free as well.

How do you follow your soul's purpose? You start with stillness, you start with introspection, you start with listening to your instincts, your intuition. I often think of my instincts as Truth attempting to make a connection—a soul connection—with my human mind. You have to be still to hear your soul speak to you. What brings you joy? What brings you peace? What could drive you each day to become a better version of yourself, to become a better you? Answer these questions and you will be one step closer to identifying your soul's purpose. Matthew 16:26 NIV says, "What good will it be for someone to gain the whole world, yet forfeit their soul?"

How will you know if you are following your soul's purpose? The level of joy that you express, give away or share with others will be a key measure of how close you are to following your soul's purpose. Does what you do nourish your soul? If not, reexamine your soul's journey. You cannot give that which you are missing in your own life. Only from your abundance can you give. Remember that your dreams are meant for you. Never quit on them, never give up on them, it is your soul whispering to you to join in the dance of life.

## Living My Soul's Purpose

I have had the privilege of working in multiple settings as a family physician and have been blessed beyond measure by all the rewards of serving thousands of individuals from all walks of life. Being part of bringing a new life into the world or calling the time of 'death' when another soul transitions into the next is simply some of the high and lows of being a physician. It would repeat my training all over again to relive these experiences because I have been given the opportunity to play a significant part in the lives of these families and play a supporting role. I have wondered though how such an altruistic profession could create an institution to devours its own, causing an average of one physician suicide per day.

There are undoubtedly belief systems that we need to address as a profession which makes it punitive for clinicians to seek help for their own psychological well-being, contrary to the very same advice that we give to our patients. Who cares for the sufferings of the healer? And many times I have asked myself, where is the family in family medicine? With the booming patient population and the ongoing shortages in the physician workforce, there is increasing pressure to see more patients for shorter periods of time. For this and many other reasons, the burnout of physicians is a hot topic in all sectors in healthcare. This quagmire of circumstances compounds on the ability of clinicians to balance personal wellness with the demands of their careers. I have discovered over the past eighteen years as a physician that my soul's purpose is to heal and that I must create that patient care delivery experience for myself in a manner that aligns with my core values and centers on the well-being of the patient.

# Five Mantras

1. When you are in alignment with your soul's purpose, you will experience joy.

2. It is up to you to identify who you were authentically meant to be and give yourself permission to become that person.

3. Be the light so others can be enlightened.

4. You have to be still to hear your soul speak to you.

5. Do what nourishes your soul to identify your soul's purpose.

## What is the next best step for making the transition into living your truth?

Be still. Hear your inner spirit whisper to you. Hear your calling and take inspired action.

# EPILOGUE

Every single chapter of this book has truly been a journey of self-discovery for me. The first chapter on vision was instinctively written by that voice in my head and that always wondered if I could do such a thing as working independently for myself. I had no trouble believing that if I wanted to accomplish anything, that I could achieve it. However, I had trouble believing that if I relied 100 percent on myself, that I would be successful. Slowly but surely that belief started to fade away as I spent more time in meditation and working on my mindset. I started to see the vision that a life of freedom and self-reliance could be an exciting and prosperous adventure and not fraught with despair. This process did not occur overnight, of course. A lot of books, personal coaching, seminars, hours in reflection and meditation, all culminated in a clear vision of who I knew I was meant to be all time. A creator.

From vision to core values. We all have them, but do we live by them? Do we live by the values that truly give meaning to why we exist? Oftentimes in the course of my life as I built my career, I felt a significant amount of lack; lack of self-care, lack of personal time, lack of free time; lack of family time; lack of worship time; and on, and on and on. All in the auspices of building a career in medicine. Despite the joy of interacting with my patients, teaching my students and physicians-in-training and publishing; I started to wonder if the unending sacrifice was what it was all about; and how come after nearly two decades, I could not seem to strike the harmonious balance of a career in medicine and true inner peace and fulfillment? I felt that the truth about a career in medicine could not be fully experienced in the current healthcare environment. Why was it taking me so long to figure out a way to harmonize career with personal and family life? Or was it even possible to find that harmonious balance? Time was slipping away from me and those I loved the most became the recipients of the least of me; those I loved the most were the sacrifice of my chosen career. Pivoting to entrepreneurship and becoming an independent business created room to be me; the me that could live based on her core values. I started to feel the possibility of freedom.

As I progressed through the chapters, they allowed me to identify with who I was truly called to become. It confirmed to me that I could no longer be defined by the four walls of medicine but rather only by the limits of my own mind and creativity. I believe that as you begin your own journey into entrepreneurship you will discover limitless freedom, flexibility, and opportunities that you never could imagine. I knew that my life was more than I could see; and as I wrote, it became abundantly clear that I was born to create and develop minds and not merely regurgitate values and principles that were not mine. As I wrote, I knew I had to break free from the 'golden handcuff' of traditional medicine and discover for myself the healer within me. I discovered that I was called to heal but not in the traditional sense as proclaimed in the textbooks I read or the scientific articles I published.

My first insight into this fact presented itself initially when I crossed the stage on the day of my medical school graduation. I did not feel the sense of completion that I expected to feel. I expected to feel extreme excitement and elation, but honestly, it felt just like another day. I had no sense of having accomplished anything great. As a matter of fact writing this book feels like a greater accomplishment than crossing the stage on graduation day. Now don't get me wrong. I would do it all over again. I love the critical thinker that I have become in the process. I have had the honor to care for and be trusted by thousands of individuals. I have participated in the birth process, a significant time in the lives of hundreds of families. I could not imagine another profession that could have given me a greater sense of satisfaction or feelings of accomplishment. However, once I accomplished that I was shocked to discover that I had not reached the limits of my capacity or interest in learning. I discovered that there was so much more within me, yet unspoken, yet unseen, that I had to give to the world. I did not feel completely fulfilled. I knew I had not chosen the wrong profession; so I knew I was meant to heal in a different way.

This led me to the chapter on legacy. Mine was not to heal individuals, one at a time. I discovered as I cultivated my thinking that it was to heal the human spirit by breaking it free from the shackles of limiting beliefs. My purpose will be to use the vehicle of entrepreneurship to show women the power of God within them to become goddesses, become self-reliant, become abundant, become leaders, and thrive in all areas of their lives. Discovering my soul's purpose has definitely been a journey best described as failing forward to success. This journey began with a hunger for true joy which then exposed me to spiritual gurus like Sadhguru; success coaches like John Maxwell; a plethora of books on personal development such as *Think and Grow Rich* by Napoleon Hill; spiritual mentalists such as Neville Goddard; and many new age thinkers such as Eckhart Tolle and Gary Zukav, just to name a few. I now know that it is okay to continue searching until as Zukav says, "The personality that you are becomes the personality of the soul." So I encourage you to see yourself as the pure light that you are that came to this earth's school to live your soul's purpose; and you came only to become the best version of yourself, so that others will be inspired and will choose to live their soul's purpose as well.

# SUGGESTED READING

Fifteen years of research and ten years of personal self-development have gone into this book. Being a lifelong learner as well as an avid reader, I've actively thirsted for knowledge and material to better understand human potential and how we can tap into the power to be, do and have all that we desire. From a very young age, I truly believed that I was called to be abundant in all areas of my life and I wanted to approach this journey with flow and ease. I share with you here, in no special order, some of the sources that I recommend and that have been most impactful in my own journey to self-discovery.

*Feeling Is the Secret*, Neville Goddard

*Authentic Power*, Gary Zukav

*The Seat of the Soul*, Gary Zukav

*The Power of Now*, Eckhart Tolle

*A New Earth*, Eckhart Tolle

*Mind Power into the 21st Century*, John Kehoe

*The Power of Your Subconscious Mind*, Joseph Murphy

*The Law of Attraction: The Basics of the Teachings of Abraham*, Esther and Jerry Hicks

*Breaking the Habit of Being Yourself*, Dr. Joe Dispenza

*Battlefield of the Mind*, Joyce Meyer

*Think and Grow Rich*, Napoleon Hill

*Start with Why*, Simon Sinek

*Miracles Happen*, Mary Kay Ash

*The Seven Habits of Highly Effective People*, Steven Covey

*Things Fall Apart*, China Achebe

*We Should All Be Feminists*, Chinamanda Ngozi Adichie

*The Thing Around Your Neck*, Chinamanda Ngozi Adichie

Core Values teachings, Scott Jeffrey

# A NOTE FROM THE AUTHOR

THANK YOU.

I hope this book has inspired you as much as I was inspired to write it. I created a quick guide to this book that readers will receive as a token of my appreciation at: GoWorkforYou.com. I'd love to hear your thoughts and learn what you would like to see more of in my next edition. Finally, dear one, whatever your dreams are, see it as done, and know that you are meant to manifest them and live your best life now. Believing in you.

Kelechi A. Uduhiri, MD

# ABOUT THE AUTHOR

Kelechi A. Uduhiri, MD, MPH, MS, is a passionate physician and entrepreneur. After realizing her dream of becoming a doctor, she elated in the joys of spending time with her patients. But as paperwork took precedence, Dr. Uduhiri felt defeated. She decided to leap from within the four walls of medicine, forge an entrepreneurial career path, and focus her efforts on empowering people, especially women, worldwide. Her mission is to inspire people to tap into the greatness within themselves, to identify their soul's purpose, and to live a life full of joy and passion.

Dr. Uduhiri holds four degrees and is board certified in two specialties: family medicine and preventive medicine. She earned her doctor of medicine degree from Rutgers-Robert Wood Johnson Medical School, has been recognized as a Fellow by the American Academy of Family Medicine, and been awarded the title of Emerging Leader in Family Medicine from the Family Medicine Education Consortium. Dr. Uduhiri resides in Olney, Maryland, with her husband, Mr. Loveday Uduhiri, and teenage son, Benjamin.

Learn more at doctorkelechi.com

CPSIA information can be obtained
at www.ICGtesting.com
Printed in the USA
LVHW030820281122
733859LV00015B/1383